The Full Moon Herald

The Full Moon Herald

poems
Phyllis Klein

GRAYSON BOOKS
West Hartford, CT
www.graysonbooks.com

The Full Moon Herald
copyright © 2020 Phyllis Klein
published by Grayson Books
West Hartford, Connecticut

ISBN: 978-1-7335568-2-8
Library of Congress Control Number: 2020906915

Book & cover design: Cindy Stewart
Front cover photo: Z.H. Chen/Shutterstock.com
Author photo: Lois Tema

for Len Weisberg, my chief correspondent in all things

Contents

From the Desk of the Editor in Chief	11

International News
It Should Be Me Who Is Looking After You	15
Crossing the Waters	17
The Human Tragedy	18
Refugee Heart	19
Don't Read This Poem	21
In the Year of the Disease	22

National News
Charlottesville Nocturne	25
Plasterboard, Wood, Terra Cotta	26
Food Chain to Stardom	27
Living with Tectonics	28
Black Friday	29

Features
Opening the Beauty Cage	33
Something Besides the Bad Thing	34
Portrait of a Woman Framed by a Wreath	35
The Seconds, Minutes, Hours, Years	36
After My Friend Rosemerry Writes About Failure and Mercy	38

Weather
Try Not to Be Afraid of This Drought	43
Breath of Damnation	44
Don't Let It Burn	45
Moratorium	46
Forecast	47

Crime
Maybe It Was a Punch	51
Inheritance	52
Going Wrong	53
Waiting for the Bombs to Drop	54
Life Is Glass	55
She Was Alone	57

Arts & Entertainment
Paul Barton Plays Piano for Elephants — 61
Prepare to Be Wrong About Everything — 62
Lord of Song — 63
The Artist Marina Abramović Is Present — 64
Halls of Fame — 65

Health
He Falls Asleep in a Wooden Library Chair — 69
Ebola — 70
Disguised as an Ordinary Spoon or Fork, in a Handshake, or the Air Between Us — 71
Hardware — 72
It Was the Tide Turning — 73

Book Review
The Powwow at the Beginning of a New World — 77
Life in the Slow Lane — 78
Bringing Flowers to Iris Chang's Grave — 79

Travel
After Landing He Awoke Praying for a New Home — 83
The Wild No Longer an Option — 84
Penumbra — 85

Obituary
The Continents, Provinces, Regions of Sharon — 89
Sherman Alexie Comes to Stanford — 90
Phlebotomy — 91
Western Black Rhino, 8 Million, My Mother, 97 — 92

Opinion
A Compassionate Judge at the Veterans Court — 97
Gathering — 98
The Touch that Lights a Backburn in Your Forest — 99
Holding a Place for Human Kindness to Go — 100

Notes — 101
Acknowledgments — 104
Permissions — 105
Masthead — 106
About the Author — 107

From the Desk of the Editor in Chief

Reading the news is complicated. Sometimes it hurts. It can bring up feelings of despair or rage about the state of the world. It can numb us, make us want to give up, convince us that nothing can be done to make the world a better place.

And yet, as much as it hurts, we need to know what's going on. It's important to stay in contact with each other and with the world. And psychologists say the news itself isn't the problem, it's more the way many engage with the news: twenty-four-hour access on our screens with increasingly shocking visuals.

So how might we receive news in a way that affirms our humanity, helps us wrestle meaningfully with difficult events and truths, and invites us to be more informed, connected and aware?

Enter *The Full Moon Herald*.

Phyllis Klein, lead reporter, brings us the news of the world and re-renders stories through her powerful poetic lens. In this brilliant collection, she courageously meets the world, both terrible and beautiful, and through her poems, we meet it more wholly. She shows us that healing comes from looking into the pain, rather than turning away. It is this seeing, naming, and containment on the page that illustrates the healing process in action.

Phyllis is well versed in this process. As a trauma-informed therapist and a poetry therapist, she understands the impact of the news on our personal experiences of suffering. And so her professional skill set, combined with her considerable talent as a writer, allows her to be a unique translator of the unthinkable.

On each page, Phyllis humanizes the news and leads us toward greater compassion. For instance, her lyric journalism helps us to see Charlottesville in the wake of the neo-Nazis:

> *the trees / draped in shrouds, their offspring out gunning.*

In another poem, she brings the plight of refugees closer to home:

> *Your refugee heart / waits, displaced heart squeezed into a suitcase, / hides under the mattress.*

Though some of these poems may break our hearts, they invite us to struggle with the tough stories of our time, and in so doing, they change us and help us feel more deeply, bringing poetic elegance into the truth of our human condition.

Phyllis Klein's *Herald* is also rich with good news. In *Arts & Entertainment*, Paul Barton plays piano for elephants. In the *Opinion* section, she chronicles the story of a man who invites someone without a home to live in an elegant newly built dwelling on his hillside ranch. She finds the poetry that can be told under headings of *Weather, Crime, Health*, even *Obituary*, which is to say that for Phyllis, everything, every single thing, is worthy of poetry, and with this sensibility, she leads us again and again from the truths of the world into the truths of ourselves so that we, too, find poetry everywhere.

What I love about Phyllis' work is her willingness to unflinchingly look at the world as it is. She doesn't pretend things are better than they are. She's not afraid to go into the dark or the difficult. She's brimming with honesty, and yet, she is ever available to beauty and love and hope as they emerge naturally from the pain. She's also the master of what I like to call "The Phyllis Klein Ending," an ending that somehow manages to bring the poem into full resonance, that makes me exclaim "oh" out loud when I read it. I ever marvel at the feelings she elicits from me—gratitude, admiration, humility, vulnerability, empathy, tenderness.

William Carlos Williams' "Asphodel, That Greeny Flower" is on point for *The Full Moon Herald*. Williams, too, was honest, democratic, devoted to understanding his country and its people. "It is difficult," he writes, "to get the news from poems / yet men die miserably every day / for lack / of what is found there."

And here it is, the news, the *real* news, of what it is to be alive in our time. And in sharing the news with us through poetry, Phyllis Klein achieves what all poets attempt to do: she moves us. She brings us "the hope of understanding," and she reminds us "we can do so much more / to be relatives in the fields / of trees, beauty, / and devastation we call home."

Rosemerry Wahtola Trommer
author of *Hush* and *Naked for Tea*

International News

It was the fabric of the human world unraveled

It Should Be Me Who is Looking After You
Letters from the dead, Taiwan

Only the night before execution
are they given
a pen and paper to say
what will be unseen
for decades. He takes the pen,
writes the message
to his unborn child.
   Before long I will leave this earth.
His wife feels their child
inside her. All she knows
is his disappearance,
the emptiness.
   Alas to be unable to see you,
   to hug you, to kiss you once.
The child arrives.
Her father is part
of a flock of magpies.
   I am heartbroken,
he says. *My regret is unending.*
All she knows is her father
is not there.

All she knows is nothing.
For sixty years she knows
not a thing. Until the letter arrives.

Another takes his pen,
writes a message to his son.
   On this earth you will never
   see your father again.
His father is a tawny owl
on a blue oak branch.
   This is the saddest thing,
he tells him. The son is lonely.
   You must not
   forget your father.

This man writes to his mother.
> *Your son believes that*
> *people who die*
> *have a spirit.*

She feels him near her like a robin
flying through an open window.
> *Your son is determined to come*
> *to your side every day*
> *to keep in touch.*

She feels the draft
of wings on her face.
> *To see your peaceful eyes,*
> *to make sure you*
> *eat three meals a day.*

So many days, so many years later
the letters arrive.
The words fly off the paper
to settle on tear drops,
tiny lanterns, drifting.

Crossing the Waters
for Billy Kwok

The evening I called Hong Kong, it was warm
for February in San Francisco. You were in the morning
sun, me, in the fading light. Your voice on the phone,
not a message, such a surprise. You answered, I didn't

know what to say, as if I were in a slot-canyon on a river,
in a boat, seeing the narrows ahead, instead of on the phone.
You answered, your greeting so respectful, my canyon opened
up, changed its geography. I wish I had thought to thank you first

of all, for your article in the New York Times. How small
I still felt, and tongue-tied. But I heard myself telling you about
the poem I wrote because your words opened a channel in me.
A passage from California to Taiwan, a story about letters

from the dead. Political prisoners, executed for speaking out.
Given a pen and paper to write farewells the night before
their deaths. Their letters buried in a drawer, a cabinet,
a word-lined grave. What would it feel like to excavate such

a letter, to see your father's or grandfather's handwriting sixty
years later? I try to imagine. None of my relatives in prison,
none executed by a government for "thought crimes".
No authorities telling them to write farewells to their families.

Nothing waiting for me in a pile of papers in an office
suffused with the dust of decades. And yet—
there is no corner on the market of suffering.
I asked you who owned the letters because I needed

permission to put them in my book. Messages from a graveyard
of narrow rivers. Who owns them? Who owns anything?
From haggard landscapes to tributaries of nourishment. Imagine
the currents of words, lost for so long. And finding you,

does it give me hope? Does it heal me somehow?

The Human Tragedy

> *Dandelions...kept alive by the finest gardeners*
> *in the world who knew how to work against nature.*
> —Jack Gilbert, *"The Difficult Beauty"*

You can only avoid it for so long. Like reading a story set in
pre-war France knowing something terrible will happen to
the lovely Jewish characters. Why do you read it? When you

started it was a happy story. Good fortune draws you in.
Love starts off loudly, calling with the ecstasy of a requiem,
only you don't want to realize that beauty leads to the grief

until it happens. More and more of this these days. More of the people
gathering, the bombs gushing off, the dead and the survivors.
No need to explain what fear feels like. It's in you, it's sitting beside

you. It's in the backs of the gardeners as they bend over
the plain yellow flowers, weeding out everything else that wants to grow.

Refugee Heart

1.

Your refugee heart
waits, displaced heart
squeezed into a suitcase,
hides under the mattress.

Your exiled hands fold,
anticipate the moment
of escape, salvation to show up
down the road. Your foreign
feet take you in that direction,
carry away your refugee heart,
your exiled hands, your immigrant
eyes looking for anything familiar
on the way to the new place.
The fields you walk, ruined.

Your wanderer's legs,
your castaway chest. It's quiet
enough to hear your breath,
your footsteps, the red
cacophony of confusion and fear.

Now the smack and smash of hate
approaching. The smell of dirt.
Your desperate mouth forming
no. Your scramble to safety.
The abandoned shack.
Your arms hanging like broken
hands in a broken clock.

Your lips, your lips, waiting
for words to come.
The chambered love
in your refugee heart
holds its beats, a conductor
waiting for time to begin again.

2.

Poor refugee heart
surrounded by thorns,
forgets how to love.

Contortionist heart
tries to find its way
out of the rhetoric
of hate, dodge
the hurtling word-bullets,
the grey war machines.

Pacifist heart, how did
you get in range
of these weapons,
this mass destruction?

Cracked heart, backlit,
fleeing, borders shut,
no man's land.

Somewhere a place,
somewhere a bed,
a meal. Hungry heart.

Refuge near an ocean,
open sky. Refugee heart
in red, second hand
still sweeping.

Don't Read This Poem

Don't get me started on the news
from Iraq, from Syria, from our public schools.
It streams onto my phone: those bodies
in the streets, the snare of an automatic,
cloud of chlorine over a city,
caged face of a child watching a gun.

My country triggers its death stars
into another gash in the world for no
good reason, gets this thing going,
the way revenge makes evil the winner,
the way crazy people can buy guns
as easily as corn chips. Don't get me

started on the way we are afraid and too busy,
how the homeless mold in the street
or at the borders while we walk by,
their realm of suffering
like another kind of death star.

Don't read this poem because
it's too hopeless. Look for love somewhere
in the rubble of human behavior. Don't
let yourself be afraid even though
you feel fear as the only choice,
even though most people know right
from wrong, even though war is a beast
beckoning from a dark place.

Go out to the ocean. Bring an extra sandwich.
Learn about the jungle. Sing homage
to John Lennon. Practice laughing yoga.
Don't fall asleep at the wheel.
Don't drive around with a body
bag in your trunk. Get the oil changed.

In the Year of the Disease

After reading Joy Harjo's poem, Grace

there was nothing more to lose until
there was. It was one thing after another,
in the spring we'd hardly notice
although it went on without a second thought.
It was the fabric of the human world unraveled.
No haircuts, no friends around the table,
no doctor visits. It was going to work, buying,
selling: all lost, or morphed into sitting
in front of our machines of connection.
It was grace, had we lost her or did she watch
from her balcony as the world pitched
into a chasm of mystery and gloom? Was she
a woman, or had she shapeshifted into a dream?
A tulip or a violet open in the sun? Some
of us knew they could find her, knew the places
she liked to hang out, while others kept trying
for a glimpse, like looking for someone
or something that had died. But she hadn't.
She might have been obscured in grief,
as she could pick it up on the wind, in the sun
or stars. She might have been angry,
and had to hide with the flowers she crushed
in her fists. Maybe she was too tired
or heartsick herself for a time.
Maybe she was lost somewhere until
she could find her way. The way. The way
back from a disaster.

National News

After the killing, my heart punching

Charlottesville Nocturne

How can I say what will happen when I go to bed
tonight? After the killing, my heart, punching,

vigilant. Sleep, a memory of a memory, or maybe
real. Chest ascending, dreams fall, suspended

in darkness, deer checking the air for danger.
Memories slink around my bed, like cats

of all sizes, grooming. Late summer with its chill,
every year the same. I ready for the descent,

climb off the mountain of day satisfied or hungry.
Today, hatred loose in the streets, in the air, dropped

out of pine trees, cones, seeds in the wind. The trees,
draped in shrouds, their offspring out gunning.

We watch the rise of a tyrant. You tell me, *People
want to be good in their hearts.* I'm no longer sure,

my heart another tyrant, a grizzly, hating in response
to hatred. My bullets loaded into the sound of a scream,

muffled. Maybe we want to think we are all good
deep down. Even the Neo-Nazi wants to know he is right,

shiny-hearted, gold-plated as he is with cruelty.
Emboldened now. And me, layered with years

of autumns, in bed with horror, tracking hope.

Plasterboard, Wood, Terra Cotta

How many times a day do you hit your own brick wall?
Your insides pounding into their limitations like heat

banging up against cold. Your inability to know the future,
comprehend the past. The architecture of your skin and bones

adorning you, deterring you. Every room a bedroom with
a balcony and a seasonal view or inward facing, paintings.

Or blank. Or wallpapered, painted, muraled. Where
are your partitions? Some things remembered, others

folded up in a suitcase in a storage locker. Do you need
a remodel? The gusts of your chronology doing their damage.

There are the glass walls also known as windows.
You looking out, others looking in. Vice versa.

What do we really know of ourselves, each other?
Our boundaries so variable, thick with concrete,

or fences at the perimeters of things. Seawalls, dikes
trying to hold back the agitated deep.

The building, the taking down. The hope for understanding.

Food Chain to Stardom

The calf runs north on the expressway,
escaping consumption in a hungry city.
Taken into custody, he is dubbed Major Deegan.

Moments of celebrity in the twittering human
circus. A number of farm animals showing up
on New York streets lately, a lamb, two goats, and

now this cow child. Once rescued, they are named,
live on in sanctuary, unlike their relatives not clever
enough to escape the slaughter. Does my steak

have a name? Two years ago a bull escaped to York College
in Jamaica, Queens, was rescued. Last year,
another died on the way to sanctuary. Alone at the back
of the custom van, cold, broken.

Living with Tectonics

You peer out at the fractured world
from under the bed that didn't collapse.
Out the window that didn't break.

The dogs howl. You prayed it wouldn't
be the big one. Is it over? Your body is tight.
The air isn't the same.

You can't say why.
It is stillness after something profound.
And there they are, howling again, an aftershock.

You check yourself, no broken bones,
You rise to see what, besides your peace
of mind, has been rattled.

Smell for gas, note broken glass, refrigerator
door ajar, a mess of food spilled on the floor.
When you moved here it was paradise, palm trees,

headlands, a bay filled with sails, no tornadoes, no snow.
This wasn't the punch kind, delivered by a subterranean fist.
This one, more lurch, then twist, and then the crashing.

You sit on the floor with the books, the overturned lamp,
the ceiling dust. There are cracks on the walls that will stay.

Black Friday

Going up in smoke. How it would happen, flames,
sprinting like trees running marathons with the wind.
Like a heavy metal screech. Pounding on the door.
If you were sleeping maybe you didn't even wake up,

the fire faster, you no contestant in anything
other than living. In your little house with its garden
so dry, how the conflagration loves dehydration.
Destroying, eating, digesting everything.

The smoke. Exhaust, exhaustion. Flashes of souls
climbing out. She with dementia, he in a wheelchair.
Others in cars, surrounded by a traffic jam of flaring
bandits, breaking in. No church or mortuary to call

when the whole town is gone. Disaster takes a trip,
we are breathing in the toxic air, the fumes of her couch,
his ashes. How we are connected. Today is a Black Friday.
Yesterday the living ate turkey, thankful for a body, a mouth

that tastes. The good and the grit. The ones with houses, the ones
without. Why do I try so hard to feel the pain? Today the scorch,
the poison, washed out of the air by rain. Today, the residue,
memorials, swindle of life and death, the ones still missing.

Features

*When did you know you would
never be beautiful enough?*

Opening the Beauty Cage

Here you are living in a fashion magazine.
Here you are, a sunflower in a field of sunflowers,
faces turned away from the shadows you stand in.

On a page, in a photograph, on a billboard.
Here, on a runway, in a movie,
a high school year book, an office, a bedroom.

This is you: girl in a burkha, athlete who has to dress
as a boy. You, girl in your mother's sweaters.
You, woman hiding in baggy shirts.

Here, a flock of cranes in flight, and there
a murder of crows. When did you know you would
never be beautiful enough?

Something Besides the Bad Thing

> *And sometimes...*
> *I run to the closet.*
> —Rosemerry Wahtola Trommer, *"Dear Rumi"*

This time, no old coats, no boots.
She huddles in the closet
naked and cold with a vine
growing over her skin,
anesthetic, a part of her.
Another way to be buried.

A song her fingers
feel but her body too cold,
too stiff. Closet song.

Something bad is stuck,
stuck in memory and body,

fixed in breath and temperature.
Something wrong, lonely,
she needs the closet darkness,
expanding vine, and her wrapped-up
hair to hide under. If she sleeps,
it will be stiff ragged escape,

the kind to jolt out of, encasing memories,
unwanted, and dreams, unbearable.
The song inside the space, slow tumble of piano
notes and a voice, no words. Suspension.
Nothing else.   Waiting.   She is waiting
for something besides the bad thing.

Portrait of a Woman Framed by a Wreath

Who comes closer? Who doesn't?
That head of hair, a billion strands,
thickets of skinny dark
skyscrapers in a hectic skyline.
Who notices that little brown ear,
the way it hugs her soft neck?
The white dress folded onto dark skin.
Come over, she says,
I have something to say.

The way her frame flowers around her.
Her anatomy, the scaffolding holding
her in and up, but not quite.
Who leans in? Who turns away?
Her tenement bouquet.
Framed. Supported. Permission
for her to stare without fear.
I see you. She shows up, she matters.
Enclosed in a wreath of peonies,
sunflowers, satisfied birds.
Who covers their eyes?

Plenitude, like that hair, meteoric pieces
of wildflower fringe. The rest of her
crackly clean. The blooming
of her world. *My best is what's to come.*
No fear, no difference. Same
as anyone, but not really.

You wouldn't know me.
Body hidden in riches, preserved
in beauty. Stage and actor.
Secret blueprints hidden below
flower petals. Under a mantle
of natural beauty, a midsummer
structure of her own desire.
Come and get it, but not really.
Who hangs her on the wall?
Who believes her?

The Seconds, Minutes, Hours, Years
for Angela

1.

They reconnect, finding the suitcases of their friendship
under their beds, not even dusty, locked, or aged, unlike their
wrinkles, limps, their dreams, their greying fears.

What is packed away gets opened, memories reaching
into the air for breath, old photographs of airports, knapsacks,
starry picnics, children giggling. Confidences.

Twenty years later, they're hiking up the mountain together again,
the golden hills roll on, as if they were a dream or a painting
or a poem, when truly, it is epiphany.

2.

And the loss. The car-keyed, moneyed, sock-littered path
leading into the blurry forest. The slipped-away, run-away
train of their lives leaving them behind on the tracks in just

their underwear. The way they had to numb themselves to make
it. All those feelings crouched somewhere. Love, in hiding,
sunning at the table for awhile, too hot, too cold.

They didn't lose an arm, a leg, or a foot, but still something
pierced inside, or burned. Their bodies a repository for
the clandestine scars. The ailments they gain. That don't leave.

3.

They find comfort in picking up the straps where
they left off. The same groove in their shoulders. Plans for
more time together. Resurrection, a cherishing of old

afflictions, an understanding. Change is possible.
And how do we connect?
Is it something in the light, the iridescence of the air, the skin?

A shared trouble, a chemical spilling its mysterious scent
around us. The lavendered, rosemaried, citrus-blossomed
lane, escort to friendship. The weedy, cindered street downtown,
silence, relationship lost, maybe, or only in the dark, in wait.

After My Friend Rosemerry Writes About Failure and Mercy

I write back to tell her
about the Brass Band revival
in Yarrabah, Australia. How Anglicans
dragged Aboriginals over to their mission
and forced them to labor in the 1890s.
How their children got yanked off
into dormitories, stripped
of their language and culture
like saplings with the wrong kind of bark.

Again, this white failure to understand
how the harness of racism
holds us all in a world without mercy.
Again, this felling of trees
in a forest already depleted and suffering.
Rosemerry, I say, *I couldn't ever believe
in a journey from revulsion to hope.
But look,* I say, *but look,
right here in the New York Times,
even this story has one slice of sun
in the chapel of despair—the Brass Band.*
Listen, you can hear it as background
for Christian hymns, its instruments
able to withstand humidity
and heat, the music shimmying up tree trunks
into bluesy sky, unable to be enslaved.

And here is the band coming
out of its silence of fifty years.
Here is Greg Fourmile on euphonium
and Paul Neal, tenor sax,
didn't know how to clap to rhythm,
let alone make music. Here are
the school kids and the grandmothers of Yarrabah
doing the best they can
to take the beat of healing into their hearts and ours.

They play for us, for everyone
who wants pride to replace shame,
for the terrible things we have done
and had done to us, and the need to go on.
For the meanness of power
and the sirens of greed.
For the insistence on healing,
the reforestation of what has been cut
but not destroyed.

Weather

the earth begs
the sky to squeeze a few drops
out of its mouth

Try Not To Be Afraid of This Drought

The only place I have to hide is…inside my poems.
—Ocean Vuong, interview in *Split this Rock*

So many clouds
and the feeling of rain.
But nothing pours.

Everything shrivels.
So dry, the earth, begs

the sky to squeeze a few drops
out of its mouth. So dry,
trees gasp, roots split

into parched cracks.
We hide, thirsty, inside this poem,

only words to drink.
Inside this poem all the fear
in the world. And all that we lose.

Then, the oranges, juice
dripping, and pomegranates,

wild red seeds staining.
Their tree-roots beseech
the subterranean lake,

so deep, *Find me*,
sunken under, *Water me*.

So much I've lost under my skin,
down in the secret parts of me.
Some things, no return.

But to come, the smell
of rain, the rain itself, the tears.

Breath of Damnation

After the fire fractures its invisible
borders, the air going south becomes
a death powder. The Anna's hummingbirds,

white-breasted nuthatches, the western
meadowlarks all disappear as if the atmosphere
has pushed them indoors. Ominous vapors grab

oranges on their bushes, fingers visible
as ghosts in a dimly lit room. The sun, our lady
of perpetual light, glares through a haze,

murky blue. Nothing wet. Or shiny. The dirt
tries to move, no wind, no dust, only rocklike
rusty brown with cracks. Everyone knows this

feeling, a drought, field drained of water,
perdition place of nightmares. Here it is: our
dread of Hades, right outside the window,

real enough to taste, to smell.

Don't Let It Burn

> *Let the lion*
> *house burn so that the roaring and burning*
> *will be heard together*
> —Linda Gregg, *"The Resurrection"*

The heat will rise in the kitchen, will free the lion
from its cage, combust the woodlands, set the fumes flowing.

Don't let the beast go on its rampage, ash getting into your lungs, disaster
in your chest—the place hearts reside, what moves in sleep. Where are

cooler heads to stop the danger in the air, the heat, the bombs?
Who will listen? Lightning strikes dried out wood,

innocent force merciless in its ignorance. Or a person, deliberate,

deranged. Where is the wise hand familiar with taming, not hopped
up on attack? Someone to understand the inferno.

What you want isn't always what you get, my mother would say as she
turned her back on me, her legs moving down a hallway into a room

in her own private smoke-gutted house. No resurrection comes from this
kind of burn. And this fire, even the sky incinerating.

Moratorium

I long for lachrymose, for the beggar in a dog's eyes.
I'm yearning for rain in deluge or drizzle, liquid as in laments.
A thousand purple umbrellas as they float over my city.

Where does it hide, this sorrow? In a secret room above
my shop? In a place a thief wouldn't find?—behind
a wall, under a stone in the dirt? This numbness.

Memories too barbed to touch. This sadness. I can feel it
brim in my exhausted eyes. Brim for my neighbor's mottled
mind—she bangs on my door, conspiratorial, insists her sweet

husband of fifty-six years plans to kill her. Brim for the children
kidnapped over an address, their only crime, a thirst for safety.
Sobbing seems appropriate. Such a luxury, release the ache, water

my dehydrated lawn. For the heat, and its cousins, flood, fire,
pollution. For bullets. For childhood. I could go on. The newspaper
should be too wet to read. Hurricane Phyllis. Broken up
over the ocean, drifting away.

Forecast
>*for Mark*

1.

January now, and finally the rain. Finally the end to smoke-filled,
smog-filled air. The finality of dark days, short exclamations

of grief. Storms headed east, spreading the flame of weather over
the land. How the earth gets covered with it. As if the sky knows

our troubles down here, takes a stand in extremes. Keeps
the sign language coming. The believers, the unbelievers

see the signs they want to see. But everyone notices ruin.
And anyone in the path of a conflagration knows terror. And too much

cold together with too much warm spells out the end of permafrost.
The garden burnt out, then flooded after the rain. The city under water,
buildings filled with fish. Divers searching for artifacts.

2.

We wait to hear about your prognosis, the echocardiogram, the MRI.
It's winter, rain again. And wind. Blustery as the valve gusting

in your chest. Your sternum cracked, they'll go in there for the leaking valve.
You're preparing for it, now that you've realized the science of it.

The risk for incident. All that needs doing, filling out the endless forms,
research, replacements for you at work. In the heat of it, the going-under

undergoing of it. In you it's all heart now. Life organized around befores
and afters. You wait at the hospital entrance, dignified, terrified, ready.

Crime

A dream as it shatters

Maybe it Was a Punch

starting with a line by Parker Palmer

Rage is one of the masks that heartbreak wears,
    with its grimace, the acrimony of bitter melon,
sneer of raw meat on bone. You wear it for self-harm,
    or to wound another. Look through its windows
at the other masks around you, masquerade but no party,
    scorched mouths, smoldering self-defeats.

Who broke your heart? And how? Did they have
    you, then hate you, punish you, leave you alone
for too long, until you cried, starving, into your pillow?
    Did they wire you with shame? So many ways
to be fragmented. So many ways to be sold, taught,
    bullied into heartbreak. Maybe it was a war inside or

outside the window, a disease, an accident, a crime
    that did it to you. Maybe it was genetics, depression,
a violation. The blistering capacity of humans to burn
    each other. Then the masks to cover our wretchedness.
Sorrow mask, grey smudged, lachrymose. Pretend mask,
    empty eyes. Vigilant mask, startle mask, blue frozen mask.

Broken heart, show us your face. Come out of hiding
    if you can. It is the way, the only way, the long way back.

Inheritance

When she hears him say he learned the world isn't safe
because his parents came out of the camps.

She finally feels the explosion of this in her blood. She had told herself,
the place she grew up so far away from there, her parents never

there either. Home was Brooklyn, was lower Manhattan. They married,
escaped with her to the suburbs. Safe streets to walk in the sun.

On their bodies, new clothes, new shoes on their confident feet. Waiting
for the bad thing to happen. The way her grandfather waited for

immigration to bang on his door, deport him, every day of his life
in this country. Her grandmother's stories, hiding under a sheep's belly

to escape the pogrom. That wasn't anything to do with now. And it wasn't
the camps. Because she had to lie to herself. Everyone did. She is away

from her birthplace, her life is her own. But every day now, for years, she wakes
up with the dread. Surely she's going to die. Every day. She can feel it.

The betrayal, nowhere to run. Her mother, now the enemy. Her father,
the helpless one whose dark side unfurls. As if her home were a camp

that nobody noticed. Like there was barbed wire, surrounding that house.
This thing, so big, so impossible to imagine even when it's happening,

is still alive. Like the monster's eye in the horror movie as it stares into
you. The things she doesn't want to feel, barreling through her.

Going Wrong

In the news, a Mexican couple, deported for telling the truth.
Branches crashing. What is the truth? Two hundred miles north,
in a comfortable home a woman tries for sleep, hunched over

the roulette wheel of her brain, waiting for that light, definite
as the traffic light at the intersection of health and illness.
Which way to turn? The light, equivocal yellow, the misery of waiting

for it to pass. The aches, cramps, the fever. Bark peeling
off the tree. She can't eat. At the table, looking at the beautiful
food, how it torments. Laboratories, technicians. Red pills,

yellow pills, green, even purple pills, which to take? Stethoscopes,
x-rays, needles. Fear and its cousin dread making faces
at the table. The wrong station on the radio, wrong as poison.

The Mexican couple banished, on the wrong list. Trying to come
clean, get legal after twenty years in the community. She reads
about them, laments for them. Years of terror. Their kids

severed from them now, branches cut off their tree-limbs.
The couple unable to earn even fifty dollars a week
back in Mexico, not their home. Waiting for her news

in the doctor's office, like a potted shrub waiting
for rain. The banishment, displacement of illness. How it pulls
you from the roots, out of your life. The mind spins it over

and over like a centrifuge at the lab. It's as bad as listening
to the news. Will she believe it? Is she just uncooperative
when the doctor tells her, *do this or die*, when she wonders,

Is he right? No trees outside the window. And she can't listen
any longer. Only music, and no reading, news too infuriating,
her inadequate heart. And the couple kicked out,

back in a homeland that isn't their home. Lies, fever, injustice.
For what? The body remembers, the body takes it in. The gut,
the head, the spine. Asking and asking for the reason.

Waiting for Bombs to Drop

> *Imagine how impossible it would be*
> *to live if some people were*
> *alone and afraid all their lives.*
> —Jack Gilbert, *"Games"*

I didn't mean to, but I did it. Opened a door into
a dark place. Where people need to claw for their

lives. I felt it. Why someone would hate them, see them
as things, worse than *filthy animals*. Want to get

rid of them, enslave them, torture, murder them. As if
I were there. I opened the gate into despair and it

flooded me, left me gasping on a rubbled shore,
the sky beaten blue, black, purple. My bones almost

broken. Witnessing in every direction, watching for
the angry mob to throng around me. The scent of guns.

I was in the middle of it, enraged. Waiting for the police
to come, throw me into a jail, a camp, a barren place

in the dust and wind. Not meaning to at first, now
I wanted to feel it. The children, infected, dying. Wails

of despair. So hungry. The parents, feverish in fear.
Standing at the ocean figuring if jumping in would

be the best way to die. The world closing its doors, windows
slamming shut. I had to retreat before I was annihilated,

before I forgot about beauty or kindness, how
an orchid blooms in my living room.

Life is Glass

*There are so many fragile things, after all.
People break so easily, and so do dreams and hearts.*
—Neil Gaiman, *Fragile Things: Short Fictions and Wonders*

Breaking: Buzz of a bone fractured, burst
of a bowl hitting the floor, boom of a heart splitting.
Please like me. A dream as it shatters.
Please think I'm good. Whistle of a word
as it severs from itself into the air.
Of a scream demolished.

Moments of breaking: Hand over the mouth,
gagging, pushed into a room, door locked from
the inside. Parties, drinking. *Why did I do that?*
The seconds it takes to get lost. Smash
of consciousness as it disappears.
Disillusion's waking croak. *Where are my clothes?*
Fragmentation into terror.

How it happens: remembering, forgetting.
Was I drugged? After school, at a party, pungency
of impact, taste without permission. No proof.
In the sacristy, in a back seat, a hotel
or a bedroom, *did it happen?*

Breaking: dust of collision, whiff of dreams
burning, nightmares strike, cymbals snarl
in the brain. *I'm repulsive.* Floating above it
all in a disappeared body.

Why she didn't tell: Pretend. It didn't happen.
No one will swallow it. He threatened,
laughed, was stronger, bigger. *It's my fault.
They won't believe me.* Pretend.
Have to see him sneer. Hide it.

What happens next: Cracks. Panic,
a plane taking off in the gut. Armor, as involuntary
as neurons saying run but all there is
is a wall. Looking ok, nobody knows. *Get over it.*

What is PTSD? The thing that won't leave, the image,
the smell, the taste that's a plague.

The crush of shame. Lack of sleep. *When is it over?*
Feeling it, numbing it. Not understanding yet
that greatness can come from damage.

She Was Alone

for Jeni Haynes

She was alone like an iceberg, but not too frozen
for her father to hurt. He assaulted her at age four almost
breaking her. Her body, a crime scene. Her mind, a disjunction.

Every day of her childhood. We know about it now because
she went to court. She was alone like a volcano on a fault
line, sitting there facing him, barbarian in a chair. Enjoying

her affliction. A gargoyle. He's going to prison now. She did
the impossible. Didn't erupt or sink him with an icy gash to his side.
Didn't smack him in the face. Found a detective who believed her.

A detective who can cry. She made an army, a republic of her, to stay real
while her criminal father tortured her. There are Muscles and Erik
in charge, but it's a democracy, a nation of her. *Alters, fragments, back*

room boiler boys and girls and notgirls. Voting on every single
important issue. Symphony testified first. Still four years
old. Remembering everything in detail. She was alone like

a seed planted in a vast empty desert. Until the others,
so many she would never be alone again, surrounded
by their palm fronds, cassia bushes, cactus guards, soothing aloe veras.

Her body a crime scene, what he did to her, how she paid with her organs
in ruins, no babies ever for her. He is going to prison for a long
time, her father. And everyone will know what he did.

How he violated her territory. He told her she was ugly, every
day he tried to ruin her. Tried but couldn't. He was a giant next to her
meager body. Bathroom tormenter. How she fought him, her beautiful

enduring, backboned, spirit. What he would never see on her cold
wounded skin. Excellent, breathtaking, outstanding beauty, had to go
under cover, beneath her waterline to the vast hidden underside.

Residence of power. She opened the door for other split
people to have their days in court. We bow to her, association of Jeni,
society, territory, unionized, incorporated, ablaze.

Arts & Entertainment

Today I learn we come from stardust, you and me,
every atom in our bodies from a star exploded

Paul Barton Plays Piano for Elephants

The piano, fountainhead to a congregation
of sick, abused, retired elephants, a man's hands
skim the keys. Animals stop, listen, flap ears.
Reach trunks around to sniff aura of the instrument,
aspect of the man. Elephants straggling about, free
now, shielded. The piano, sitting on the dirt in a park,
surrounded. Picture it: man playing Bach to a creature
large enough to kill him, stomp up his keyboard.
The elephant stands transfixed.
The man gives bananas at first to make a good impression.
It helps them memorize his smell, connect him to the sounds.
He walks with a group sometimes, the blind ones. Even if they
knew where the piano once got its keys, what would
they do? Crush it? This cruel, splendid coincidence.
This Moonlight Sonata under the stars, these behemoths swaying.

Prepare to Be Wrong About Everything

like the Nazis were wrong about the Jews.

Last night I went to a concert, *Violins of Hope*.
The restored instruments had made it out

of the camps, were played by fine musicians.
A mezzo soprano sang a specially composed
song cycle about the violins, their players.

How the Nazis liked good music, found
the acoustics worked best in the death-shower
rooms. Imagine a prisoner playing his violin

in that blank black place. I was wrong not to want
to go to the concert, because it moved me, was sad,
of course, but also compelling. The violins, and even

a cello, escaped from the camps, their owners probably
gone by the time liberation came. Survivors
went back in and freed the instruments. That took courage.

Going back to the scene of bleakest black. Later,
a man in Israel decided to find those violins, restore them.
Found human ashes inside one. Served as a reminder

for *Never Again*. But even that feels wrong just now.
And it's wrong to avoid trauma, because it will find
you wound up tight like strings over a bridge, into a pegbox,

down to a tailpiece. I was prepared to be overcome,
but the notes tried to save me from the dark. Appearances
are deceiving. The music lives on. And Judaism lives on,

although I don't like religion anymore. I think it's wrong
to persecute anyone, but I do it, too, especially to myself,

which is really wrong. This damage, it plays and plays.

Lord of Song

with apologies to Leonard Cohen

Leonard, lucky you missed this,
left us just as the music took
its minor slip, you missed this ugly,
damaged time. When faith, they say, is
strong, but tied up to a dining room chair.
No need to cut any Samson's hair,
it's all handcuffs and thrones now.

It's all fear and hate, lies and cries,
the victors march across our stage,
but what's really going on below,
they never show us, do they? And
what's this faith, this Lord of Song,
is he watching now, is he even there
as innocents go down to the valley
of their shadows?

And who remembers dear Anne Frank,
Trayvon Martin, Emmett Till?
The best among us, flanked by tears,
not coming back, and still the deaths
continue. What's important now: your shade
of skin, the soldier, how you stand your ground.
Keep the other out, they shout and shout,
make sure the bathroom door stays shut, take
back what's been won, keep your gun.
It's a frigid, and a fractured alleluia.

The Artist Marina Abramović Is Present

Pain is the stone that art sharpens itself on time after time.
—Heather Rose, *Museum of Modern Love*

One at a time, seven hundred fifty thousand people sat in front
of her at the New York MOMA over three months,
no speaking, only looking into her eyes.

Many of them moved to weep. Many of them in line for hours,
even camping out on the sidewalk for the next day's chance.

Getting to know each other. In another poem, I outlined the star
she cut into her belly more than once. And the performance
when she could have been murdered, the way people are pernicious.

So terrible, I forgot about the love part. Something in her gaze,
magnet drawing crowds into her room. Sitting on a chair, motionless

for seven hours. Seduction into self-knowledge?
Lure of supposed intimacy? Something real, true?
I wasn't there. I imagine her from photographs, all in blue,

red, then white. Each month a new color. For the same
sameness of the days. Repetition making its impression.

Looking into me, whatever she sees reflected, reversed,
vision as a ball we toss, a loop of connection, a love letter,
a recognition. How long would I last under the sun lamp

of her eyes, the spell of her intensity? I want it to be love,
to be hope. Why can't she let herself take a bathroom break,

get a lunch and a stretch? Wouldn't that be love? If it's the stone,
the sharp one, she's sharpening her body on it. If it's our nature,
our lesions, their healing, and her, love's daredevil, siren of eyes.

Halls of Fame

Today I learn we come from stardust, you and me,
every atom in our bodies from a star exploded, a super
nova living inside your skin, my heart. Inside Brian
May's astrophysicist hands playing juiced-up guitar
for Queen. The star bomb plunging into Joni

Mitchell's fingers holding the pen that wrote about
the billion-year-old carbon, voice showing
the way to the Woodstock she wouldn't be able to attend.
A way for the universe to know itself. A star in the hustling
heavens for each human on earth. The stars that died

so you could live. Spread their carbon into our apple
pies, back in the garden, nitrogen on your oak tree,
calcium in my teeth and bones, the oxygen in Joni's lungs
when she sang, *you are golden*. Music, sweet headliner
in the stardust parade, propeller of our species, epigenetic picnic.

Phosphorescence-streaming glitter on headliners at the Apollo—
James Brown, Diana Ross, the Roxy—Frank Zappa, Bob
Marley, echoes of guitar, like race-car meteors, ascending.
Leading the parade, Freddie Mercury, falling off the movie
screen into star sprinkles in my eyes and ears, I'm surfing

into proximity of brilliance, Freddie, who donated
songs to the world, his sun bulldozing the stage, tunes battering,
thrashing in his feet, legs, body of a man on fire, halfway up
there already. These songs, most of us know the words and melodies,
blazing, shooting, championing, rocking. Perhaps this is why

I find myself weeping over the baby bok choy at the Farmers
Market today, loving everything, the farmers, shoppers, the vegetables
themselves, the stardust that made me, the garden that grew us,
will we ever get back?

Health

*That return
to equilibrium after a hurricane
or a debacle of illness*

He Falls Asleep in a Wooden Library Chair

and in a pasture finds his old dog no longer dead.
He prances with the dog, can run with ease again.
The trail is rough, but not too steep. The dog licks and the sun
shines from its house while flowers forget that it's winter.
They both whimper as he starts to drift back to the pain
of the waking world, where fluorescent lights shine
and his glasses lay folded on the table.

Ebola

He had arrived alone to the treatment center. In an ambulance.
Had to wait for the nurses to decide if he were contagious.

Have you been throwing up? they asked from across the room.
Plenty, he said. *Has anyone died in your house?* He nodded. *Three.*

Someone came in wearing one of those space suits to help him to a bed.
No touch allowed. He was alone and small, so sick and so small,

all of nine years. He was scared and missed his parents,
and his even-smaller sister. He was the last one left. No one

to check on him except the journalist covering Liberia who happened
to be at the clinic when he arrived; soon she also left him.

His small dark body curled into itself. No touch allowed.
No childhood left whichever way he went.

Disguised as an Ordinary Spoon or Fork, in a Handshake, or the Air Between Us

Highly magnified, they look like many-handled nerf balls,
stealth drones, jumping from one set of human lungs
to the next. Rabid science fiction monsters

on a tainted spaceship. Can you say *pandemic*?
Can you stop reading all the emails, the warnings
everywhere? This fearsome, this formidable virus
we have to dance with. Our hands now our enemies,

instruments of possible extermination. No touch, and forget
about a hug, this is the new solo tango. To be healthy
is to wash all digits for twenty seconds while singing

the chorus of *I Will Survive*. And don't touch doorknobs
anymore. What is it about contact between fingers and face
that is so irresistible? And human contact, how we notice its absence

as all gatherings drain away and friendships go behind
a curtain six feet wide. We saw the videos from China,
but we're not used to this here. The new thing

now, social distance, translates to home alone with
your computer, phone, and wet wipes, if you can find
any. Isolation. Let's hope for a new family

in the White House. Let's hope for more music,
more poetry. Shared rooftop dinners from a safe
distance. Neighbors with food offers for the at-risk

delivered to the door. And best of all, a vaccine
that can step on Corona's toes, kick it out of the dance
hall forever. And how do you know if you'll be the mild

case, the one you dream can give immunity, or the worst
option, and no time and maybe no ventilator to prepare for the end.
This breath you used to take for granted, is it cancelled?
This ambush, this wretched air.

Hardware

It might seem to you that your machines are just as important
as your defeated heart, taking its beating too seriously
or not seriously enough. Those machines you depend on can
crash, go on life support, data lost in a cave-in as the heart

knows too well. Your hard disks corrupted with error messages.
The heart recognizing, goes on trying, you looking for what's deeper,
explorer excavating for the tunnel to your pristine self. That can
never be corrupted. Hiding.

The heart is muscle, flexing into the decades of its drum rolls.
You believe in the power of fixing, tech support, software cleaning.
Lowering cholesterol, reducing inflammation. It's becoming almost
the same to you. Your heart is echo, the sound of a trillion memories

traveling to your brain in a suitcase labeled *The Past*. Sound of a car horn
blasting, a waterfall surging, an orchestra playing a bolero. The heart
is wind, passage of time, silicon chips flying into the night sky. The next
day could be sun or torrents, still you go on, the things about you

in the files searching for immortality, if only they can be saved.

It Was the Tide Turning

It was the slip of paper he left
on the table with the note
saying where he'd be and when
he'd return. Just the basic
information about a day set
up to thrum like any other.
And the heart he'd drawn
at the end, beating like
a metronome in a kitchen,
practicing its rhythms
of pour and stir as she lit
the gaslight on the stove, waiting
for the blue flames to jump
up, embrace the pan. To fry
those eggs so the yellow
would drip on its plate
like an oil painting in progress.

It was the new blue sweater espousing
her waistline, the feel of its
luxury on arms, pliable wool.
The sleep that had called through
the night before, pulling her down
into rip tides of surrender. That return
to equilibrium after a hurricane
or a debacle of illness, when decay
freshened, sunlight rose in the windows
of her body, and she opened them,
especially her eyes.

Book Review

*Hold me in your branches
and I will speak to you*

The Powwow at the Beginning of a New World

after Sherman Alexie, "The Powwow at the End of the World"

I am told by you that I must forgive and so I shall after
you make time go backwards. I am told by you that I must
forgive and so I shall after the floodwaters of your behavior flow

the other way and the women waiting at the mouth of the river
of rage see their shame float by. I am told by you that I must
forgive and so I shall when the deep salty waters, tears of the women

you hurt, evaporate into the mist. How to breathe again. How to
lean on each other. I am told that I must forgive and so I shall, when the
women make a powwow at the beginning of a new world invite

everyone, every tribe including yours. Including me, a white elder.
Who wants to not be in awe of you, wants to erase
the photograph I took of you but can't. Me, a woman who can't get

your words, effigies, stories out of my neurons. I shall try to forget
your drunken father, the mother staggering out of your memoir,
the Indians you showed me how to love. Forgive me because

I can't forget. Forgive me for wanting to tell you the way I feel,
the stories about why you can't do this to me, and why you have
done it. What am I going to do with the poems I wrote for you

now that they are tainted by the truth? And all those lost Indians
you wrote about, now you're a lost Indian running with them.
I wanted you to save me the way your writing did. I am told by you

that I must forgive and so I shall when there is no need for you to hunt
women the way you would hunt deer or fish flying free because
you are stronger, when women won't be afraid to love anyone's words

and it won't have to be the end of the world for it to happen.

Life in the Slow Lane

after reading Peter Wohlleben, The Hidden Life of Trees

Hold me in your branches
and I will speak to you
through our roots, intertwined
in our bed, our bedroom of orchids,

our kitchen window redwood, our rooms
connected like living telephone wires,
our bodies, our pheromones singing arias,
the microbes who call us home riding

on our backs into the jungle of our city.
Let us be silent like the trees,
endure pain with dignity, leafy
or bare, dressed or naked.

Be patient for the ecstasy
of life, patient for the ice, the wind,
patient for warmth. Let us give space
the way trees grow their branches

so light reaches every leaf of every tree.
Welcome cats, birds, monkeys and snakes.
Welcome. And let us endure leaf eating
pests and mammals, mold, rot, drought

and flood. Let us make seeds and cones
to fly on winds of longing, seeds to fly into us
as we hold each other, as we speak through our roots,
the soft damp sky filled with birds calling.

Bringing Flowers to Iris Chang's Grave
for Peidong Sun

You ask your friend to take you to the cemetery
in Los Altos where she is buried. To pay respects.
You are leaving soon, back to China, to your husband

and young daughter, to your work at the University in Shanghai.
It becomes night, the graveside visit slides into darkness,
a white flower bouquet aglow in your hands. To pay respect

to Iris. It's a beautiful California cemetery, a park with headstones.
Where is she in this community of the dead? Where no one can
threaten her anymore. A man thinks you want to sell him your

flowers, as you run to catch him, to ask for directions. But he
is also a visitor. When you do find her, finally, placing the blossoms
on her last place in the physical world, lingering in the ink,

the opacity, the casualty. How do you spread yourself wide
enough to take her life in? What of the gun she pointed to herself?
What really killed her, champion of human rights, she who told

the truth to a belligerent world? She who wrote *The Rape of Nanking*,
and more, oh, the sleepless nights of horror. What it means to be
Chinese in America, what it meant to be Chinese when a war

unleashed the most sinister, the wicked, the fires of battle burning
innocents in Nanking. Rape is a crime of the night. You say she
succumbed to the darkness. You visit her grave to thank her.

This is why I thank you, young and lovely, an iris flower
from a foreign place, teaching me about goodness,
about illumination to the face of grief.

Travel

Maybe he still had just enough hope

After Landing He Awoke Praying for a New Home

Fury gave him courage to climb the airport fence.
Not caring where he went, he crawled into the plane's wheel well.

He didn't want to die, only to disappear.
He felt the speed and lift off the ground, but was already detached

from his body. His despair floated in the icy air like someone else's frozen tears.
He fell asleep and his heart went into hibernation,

a fifteen-year-old Arctic heart still beating at 35,000 feet.
Maybe the anger saved him, like a blanket pulled close to his skinny body

that kept some heat in. Maybe he still had just enough hope.

The Wild No Longer an Option

How to hold a monkey's hand: place your
left hand under its palm, stroke with your other
hand. Remember, this monkey has lost
its mother. Look at both sides of the hand,
nails so much like yours, palms and fingers
you want to cradle but others are waiting.

The monkey won't look you in the eye.
Later will grab its meal from your hand,
crimson or yellow, orange or green.
Of course it will prefer sweet watermelon to
the tang of spinach, but once the fruit
is gone, will crunch the greens until they disappear.

Know that these monkeys, the spiders, capuchins,
the howlers, are here in a cage waiting for their
murdered mothers to return. In a cage for safety,
too innocent for the wild. Remember, if you can,
what it feels like to be trapped, abandoned, alone.
To be little, to be spooked, shivering eyes. Imagine

swinging from a tail you will never have. Remember
that innocent hand in yours, that creature so much
your relative. And you, also longing for a mother.

Penumbra

> *Because in this world*
> *you have to decide what*
> *you're willing to kill.*
> —Tony Hoagland, *"Candlelight"*

Saving yourself means getting the glasses
that let you watch the moon cover the sun.
You drive or fly to the dot on the map.

For a couple of minutes it's night, then day again.
You imagine all this. Alone, just you and the dark
that is light. The moon, now a black song

backed up by blazing jazz, surging jazz,
drunked-up jazz. It won't last. Like your parents
smiling in the camera's flash, did they decide to try

killing you breath by breath? Or were they living
in their own night's gloom, and you, planet
of heartbreak orbiting skies clouded with shame.

Then the girl at the sleepover you thought would stay,
curly hair backlit by a flashlight. How the lover
climbed over your being and left you. When

the spheres of your body began to inflame. Saving
yourself means looking through grief's lens.
Its totality, wax and wane, a shadow, its translucence.

Means feeling the moon start to rise. The earth turn.

Obituary

*What did you know when
you couldn't detect another scent like
yours anywhere, anymore?*

The Continents, Provinces, Regions of Sharon

Sharon died, the cancer slowly finding the core of her.
So many years of living with it, over. The drugs, hospitals,
doctors' offices. Done. Sharon died, and a great blue
whale swam into the sky, hung on a red-tinged cloud over

the continent Masterpiece above the ocean of Nepenthe
during the time of reclamation. Sharon died. And a tree
grew in the dominion of shadows, its bark, fingers
with crystal afterglows, branches alive with creatures'

long tails, from the province Mortality, friendly gloom.
Sharon went away. And a tiger sat in a mountainous night,
head in a conflagration, no pain, glinting at the stars.
And a boardwalk led to a tree, on the left a great lake, profusion

of life, on the right a desert, brown ghost limbs. Of course
she is there with the whale, tiger, boardwalk, trees.
She died. But don't be disheartened. You knew
her ready smile, tempting spark, all the ways she recovered.

Sherman Alexie Comes to Stanford

for Greg Kimura, 1956-2017

You would come to this, I know, ready to receive the news
and weather from him, "part-time" Indian, full-time writer,
husband, father. The way he would make you laugh with the twist
of his edge, his "you liberal white people" jabs, the Indian

jokes, the accents, how he gets all the tribal Stanford students
to stand up so he can tell them how proud he is of them.
He glows down from the stage. Maybe it would help
you forgive yourself to know that he swears too, or maybe

it would offend you. I'm not sure. He says stories are the thing
for us humans, and you know that, too. In a poem he says,
"I always knew grief was a storyteller." I feel you in the hall
with us, you're a tree with birds singing in your branches.

You're with us when we go up to have our book signed
and tell him we love him, kind of trite, but the truth. You'd
want to know that he says he edits his poetry a lot, even him,
damn it. Oh sorry, pretend you didn't hear that.

And sorry you missed him, Greg. You would have soaked him in.
Here's your story: You are with the autumn leaves drifted from
your tree now, piled up, then spread into the world by winds.
When you left, you were almost air already, but still shining. Like always.

Phlebotomy

For Jack Ridl

He introduces himself just before the needle,
My name is Rodel, he says, *after my dead brother
Rodelio*. I offer my arm and the blood slips
into his vials, two needed this time. *My brother
died at three months*, he says, *fifty years ago in*

the Philippines, my only brother. I don't usually watch
the red liquid from my body course into the tube. Today
I want to see it fill up the ampules that will bear it to the lab.
Is it thick as the blood between these Asian brothers? I ask
him, was there a reason he told me this today? How he

couldn't have known about you, your also-lost brother,
the poem you sent me just an hour before. Your brother dead
in the womb so many years ago. The brothers neither of you
would ever have. Both of you, only sons. Rodel, thirty,
you past seventy. How the two of you became friends

through my blood. My blood on the way to the lab, coagulated
into numbers of discovery, useful information, possible
hope. Your brothers' hemoglobin in your bodies forever.
Blood brothers. Stories of possibility lost in the dirt
of death. Sports never played, careers never found,

no teaching how to throw a ball, how to lose
your homework. How you both live on in their shade,
their voices whispering about what could have been.
My blood on the way to its future. All blood,
transfused with the ways of our losses, our passage.

Western Black Rhino, 8 Million, My Mother, 97

1.

The night the last western Black Rhino gasped,
the full moon held vigil in a place where several
mahogany trees wailed up from the flat earth along
the river Nyong. A sub-species disappears,

this one already a living fossil born eight million
years ago, no match for the millions of dollars its horn
could call in. Still holding on while people pillaged.
Mud loving, mistakenly thought to be near sighted,

clumsy-fast, big old herbivore, can't play your horn
no more. The night you died out
forever, why didn't I feel it? Where is your grave,
where are your mourners? Did you know what

was coming, your thick hide craving cool mud
you couldn't find? What did you know when
you couldn't detect another scent like
yours anywhere, anymore?

2.

When my mother dies, will I grasp it before I am told?
Will I feel it the same way I knew my sister was hit
by an SUV and survived, because I kept thinking
about her, thinking about being run over, over

and over in my mind. Saw a bus stopped on the road in
front of me, thought, *that bus could batter me into
the pavement.* Even though we weren't speaking
and I live 3,000 miles away, I still knew.

My mother, determined, terrified.
How she could yell. Trodden on. Vindictive.
Holding out at ninety-seven. Totally debilitated,
demented. Facing extinction. I didn't want

us to end like this. Whatever was precious,
stolen. Whatever was loving, trampled.
Whatever trampled, persistent
as the beating of a determined heart.

Opinion

*And a judge can be a brother
to a man who has lost his way,
as two oak trees in a meadow
can be connected by their roots*

A Compassionate Judge at the Veterans Court

*After sentencing Sergeant Joseph Serna on a parole violation,
Judge Lou Olivera follows him into his jail cell.*

And so, when the judge
gets into the cell
with the man he has just sentenced
to twenty-four hours in jail,
the man asks, *For the whole day?*
and the judge says,
Yeah, that's what I'm doing.

Like a father who says,
He's my son and I won't see him fall.
And a son who isn't alone
locked down in the dark with his terror.

Because the judge has been to war, too,
and knows there are wounds
that aren't visible. Because the man,
two decades in the military, knows
another soldier died for him in combat,
and lives crushed under this,
and not only this.

And a judge can be a brother
to a man who has lost his way,
as two oak trees in a meadow
can be connected by their roots.
The way a man who has lost
his way can be a messenger
to remind us
there is so much more to know
about what's on the inside.

Because we are so ready
to skate on the surface
of our minds. Because
we can do so much more
to be relatives in the fields
of trees, beauty,
and devastation we call home.

Gathering

Our tree, fertile with them, red-fruited-multi-faceted
ornaments of pride. Start as lipstick red flowers
that drop into faded garlands wreathing like a collar
fallen to the floor. Red bulbs appear, harbingers
for the fruit. Hard shelled, pregnant, crimson-

seeded miracles. How did they get so large? And why
are the seeds so hard to extract? It's been a dry summer,
a dryer fall, and yet here they are, so many we have to look
for places to donate them. A homesick man named Igor,
from Armenia, once climbed the tree for some, afterwards

left a thank you note and packages of crackers and cookies
from Trader Joe's. A neighbor comes this year with two kids,
fascinated while cutting them off the branches, eager to begin
the harvest of scarlet cells called arils. Friends graciously
receive too many, send to the east coast in a box. Make jam,

bread. Put on salads. Bring to other neighbors. Everyone
set to whacking at them. Our kitchen a crime scene, splayed
with the stains of ruby-juice. Persephone visits our dreams.
She who sacrificed to give us winter, shadow days, blizzards
of rain. A cleansing. The ways we try for redemption.

The tree, a skeleton now, still a few offerings left
on otherwise vacant limbs. So many years, such faithful service.
During the dark times, beacon of magenta, of vermillion.

The Touch that Lights a Backburn in Your Forest

Touch can do that,
scorch of longing,
cleansing of heat.
You wait for
the dream
that maybe
isn't a dream.

So close, it
flickers against
your hair, ignites
your lips, kindles
the pink of imagination,
like a sunrise through
the birch trees
or a watercolor
someone paints
for you to enter.

On the verge
of a doorway,
a freedom, a love,
still innocent
but different.
You can't help
but walk into
yourself, an ocean
of sun-crazy leaves.
You vibrate in wonder,
in youth, but no longer
a child. A breeze
holds you close
as you claim
yourself, woman,
forested, liberated.

Holding a Place for Human Kindness to Go

Strangers, until the homeless man moves into the rancher's
apartment, the one he decided to build on his land,

generous with California oak woodlands, with coastal
sage scrubs. The rancher wonders, *Why doesn't everyone*

do this? He doesn't realize it is greatness to see potential when
everyone else sees menace, those immigrants invading

like Mediterranean grasses, Spanish Broom, Yellow Star
Thistle. Weed them out, those seekers, or the downtrodden

down thrusted, the ones bereft of four walls, invading the city,
choking out the libraries, the beaches. And the homeless man

who has a roof now doesn't realize his life is a poem
when he says, *living on the streets takes your dignity away.*

How his life was on the edge of felling, so much like a weed
in a garden he could pluck out himself. And now he lives

in a new home on a ranch near a person who takes a risk, digs
a foundation, offers the horses, the owls, the steelheads, also endangered.

Notes

"It Should be Me Who is Looking After You" responds to an article about letters written by prisoners during the White Terror in Taiwan. The article appeared in the *New York Times* on February 3, 2016.

"Crossing the Waters" was written during my search for copyright on the letters in the previous poem. This involved calling the reporter, Billy Kwok, in Hong Kong.

"The Human Tragedy" is one of many of my poems with an epigraph by Jack Gilbert, whose poetry I find endlessly inspiring.

"In the Year of the Disease" was written during a meeting of the "Writing for Healing" group I lead, that has been virtual since the shelter in place started. I used Joy Harjo's spectacular poem, "Grace" from *In Mad Love and War* to stimulate our discussion and generate writing prompts.

"Food Chain to Stardom" is about an escaped calf who was named after the Major Deegan Expressway in New York City, where he was found. The article was in the *New York Times*, March 19, 2019.

"Opening the Beauty Cage", "Something Besides the Bad Thing", "Portrait of a Woman Framed by a Wreath" and "The Touch that Lights a Backburn in your Forest" are poems written in response to artwork by a special yoga teacher, Janya Wongsopa.

"After My Friend Rosemerry Writes About Failure and Mercy." Rosemerry Wahtola Trommer wrote a poem based on a headline I pointed out to her. Her poem *After my Friend Phyllis Shows Me the New York Times Obituary Headline: Lou Michaels, all purpose player, dies at 80, 'missed kicks in '69 Super Bowl'* is in *Rattle.com* ("Poet's Respond," January 26, 2016). I couldn't resist writing a response. My poem is based on the article about the Aboriginal Community and its Brass Band. *New York Times*, January 24, 2016.

"Try Not To Be Afraid of this Drought" responds to an interview with Ocean Vuong. (*Split This Rock*, Tuesday, February 16, 2016).

"Going Wrong" is about an Oakland, CA couple I first heard about on the radio. *The San Francisco Chronicle's* article about them is in their December 20, 2017 issue. The other character in the poem is fictional.

"Life is Glass" is dedicated to Christine Blasey Ford and all survivors of sexual assaults.

"She Was Alone" came from watching the story on YouTube, and reading an article about Jeni Haynes online, both at *60 Minutes, Australia*, May 27, 2019. Jeni's testimony opened the way for people with dissociative identity disorder to be considered credible as court witnesses. I was lucky enough to have a colleague connect me to Jeni on email so she could read an earlier version of the poem and give me her feedback on it. I feel that we wrote it together. The term "alters," used in the poem, refers to parts of the self in dissociative identity disorders, and "fragments" are parts of the self that are not as elaborated as other alters but are still considered to be viable aspects of self.

"Paul Barton Plays Piano for Elephants" was inspired by an article in *Mother Nature Network*, August 31, 2018. Mr. Barton is a wonderful pianist living in Thailand.

"The Artist Marina Abromavić is Present" was written after reading Heather Rose's brilliant book *The Museum of Modern Love* (Algonquin Books, 2018).

"Ebola" was written after listening to a radio interview with a Liberian-American journalist.

"The Powwow at the Beginning of a New World" repeats the line "I am told by many of you that I must forgive and so I shall," which is a repeated refrain in Sherman Alexie's poem "Powwow at the End of the World." I have slightly changed the refrain.

"Life in the Slow Lane" refers to *The Hidden Life of Trees* by Peter Wohlleben (Graystone Books, 2018).

"Bringing Flowers to Iris Chang's Grave" is for Peidong Sun, associate professor of history at the Fudan University in Shanghai. I was lucky to get to know her through a mutual friend, Kirill Kalinin, when she was staying in Palo Alto as a Fellow of the Hoover Institute.

"After Landing He Awoke Praying for a New Home" is based on a story aired on *ABC News*, April 21, 2014.

"The Continents, Provinces, Regions of Sharon" is about Sharon Hoeker, who died on September 24, 2018 in Ann Arbor, Michigan.

"Western Black Rhino, 8 Million, My Mother, 97" is inspired by an article, declaring the Western black rhino extinct, in *Time Magazine*, November 6, 2013.

"A Compassionate Judge at the Veterans Court" about Justice Lou Olivera, was inspired by an article in the *Washington Post* on April 22, 2016.

"Holding a Place for Human Kindness to Go" about a homeless man and a rancher relates to an article that appeared in the *New York Times* on July 2, 2018.

Acknowledgments

Thanks to the editors of the following journals who published or will publish the work listed here, sometimes in an earlier version:

A Hundred Falling Veils, *Poetry Hotel*, and *Writer's Resist*: "Life is Glass"

California Fire and Water: "Black Friday"

Carolyn Forché Humanitarian Poetry Prize Finalist: "Inheritance", to be published in *Elusions*, Waterwood Press

Dovetails, an International Journal of the Arts, Refugees and the Displaced: "Refugee Heart"

Fischer Prize Competition 2019, Fourth Finalist: "A Compassionate Judge at the Veterans Court"

Kind of a Hurricane Press: "He Falls Asleep in a Wooden Library Chair"

Minnesota Review: "It Was the Tide Turning"

New Verse News: "My Friend Rosemerry Writes About Failure and Mercy," "Breath of Damnation," and "A Compassionate Judge at the Veterans Court."

Poetry Hotel: "Penumbra"

Portside: "Holding a Place for Human Kindness to Go"

Silver Birch Press: "Living with Tectonics" (as "Living With Geology")

Sweet: A Literary Confection, Inaugural Poetry Contest, Finalist: "Hardware"

Permissions

I wish to thank the following publishers and individuals for permission to reprint portions of the following:

Fragile Things, by Neil Gaiman. Copyright 2006 by Neil Gaiman. Reprinted by permission of Writers House LLC acting as agent for the author.

"The Difficult Beauty" from *Collected Poems* by Jack Gilbert, Copyright 2012 by Jack Gilbert. Used with permission of Alfred A. Knopf, an imprint of the Knopf Doubleday Publishing Group, a division of Penguin Random House LLC. All Rights Reserved.

"Games" from *Collected Poems* by Jack Gilbert, copyright 2012 by Jack Gilbert. Used by permission of Alfred A. Knopf, an imprint of Knopf Doubleday Publishing Group, a division of Penguin Random House LLC. All rights reserved.

Jeni Haynes, *Alters, fragments, back room boiler boys and girls and notgirls*, used with permission of Jeni Haynes.

Tony Hoagland, excerpt from "Candlelight" from *Donkey Gospel*. Copyright © 1998 by Tony Hoagland. Reprinted with permission of The Permissions Company, Inc., on behalf of Graywolf Press, Minneapolis, Minnesota, www.graywolfpress.org.

Healing the Heart of Democracy, by Parker Palmer. Copyright 2011 by Parker J. Palmer. Published by Jossey Bass, A Wiley Brand. Used by permission of Wiley Global Permissions.

Museum of Modern Love, by Heather Rose, Copyright 2016 by Heather Rose. Published by Algonquin Books of Chapel Hill. Used by permission of Algonquin Books.

"Dear Rumi" from *A Hundred Falling Veils*, February 26, 2012, Used by permission of the author.

Split this Rock, Tanya Olsen's 2016 interview with Ocean Vuong, Used by permission of the editor. https://blogthisrock.blogspot.com/2016/02/split-this-rock-interviews-ocean-vuong.html

Masthead

Publisher
Ginny Connors

Editor in Chief
Rosemerry Wahtola Trommer

Washington Bureau Chief
Paul Fericano

Editor Emeritus
Jack Ridl

Mentorship Desk
Perie Longo

Education Desk
Kim Addonizio, Molly Fisk, Victoria Chang, Carolyn Dille, Lola Haskins, Jacques Rancourt

Writers and Friends Desk
Lisa Rosenberg, J. David Cummings, Christine Holland Cummings, Kalamu Chaché, Charlotte Muse, Patrick Daly, Judy Taylor, Barbara Allen, Monica Korde, Bobby Meile, Mary-Marcia Casoly, Peter Neil Carroll, Aleta Hayes, Greg Kimura

Virtual Desk
Poetry Working Group, Claire Scott, Simona Carini, Keith Welch

Friendship and Support Desk
Carolyn Stark, Norm Weiner, Angela Kray, Rita Vrhel, Cam Vozar, Paula Koepke, Karen Levin, Shaun Phillips, Bill Reed, Sharon Sasaki

Distribution
Three on a Match—Bird and Beckett San Francisco, Cafe Zoe Poet's Night, Not Yet Dead Poets Society, Waverley Writers, Peninsula Literary, Savanna Jazz, Rita Vrhel's Living Room

About the Author

Phyllis Klein works as a psychotherapist specializing in trauma and a Certified Poetry Therapist. She has lived in the San Francisco Bay Area for over 30 years. Her work has appeared or will appear in many literary journals. She was a finalist in the Sweet Poetry Contest (2017), the Carolyn Forché Humanitarian Poetry Contest (2019), and The Fischer Prize, (2019) and was nominated for a Pushcart Prize (2018). She sees writing as artistic dialogue between author and readers—an intimate relationship-building process that fosters healing on many levels. Writing about the news is her way of taking action to counter feelings of overwhelm and loss.

www.ingramcontent.com/pod-product-compliance
Lightning Source LLC
Chambersburg PA
CBHW021117080526
44587CB00010B/553